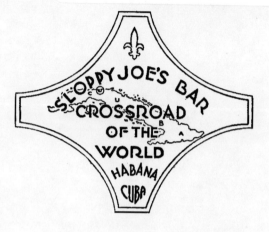

SLOPPY JOE'S BAR
CROSSROAD OF THE WORLD
HABANA CUBA

SLOPPY JOE'S BAR
COCKTAILS
MANUAL

HAVANA, CUBA

SLOPPY JOE'S BAR
COCKTAILS
MANUAL

Being a more or less discursive account of the intoxicants
served at Cuba's legendary watering hole, their formulae and
uses, together with instructions on the mixing of drinks.

by
José Abeal
Proprietor, Sloppy Joe's Bar

First published 1931
Reprinted 1932
Reprinted 1933
Reprinted 1934
Reprinted 1935
Reprinted, with additional material........................2008

Restaurant Museum books are available at quantity discounts with
bulk purchase for educational, business, or sales promotional use.
For information, please contact: restaurantmuseum@gmail.com
Please supply: title of book, quantity, how the book will be used,
date needed.

DEDICATION

In general this book is dedicated to all those who appreciate a good drink; in particular it is offered as homage to the *cantineros* of old Havana and is especially dedicated to this goodly company of master barmen and their craft.

How 'ya Gonna Wet Your Whistle When the Whole Damn Country Goes Dry?

You can never know everything about anything. Certainly not about America's relationship with alcohol, and not even, it turns out, the notion of a law which made the consumption of alcohol illegal. At midnight on January 16, 1920, the prohibition of the sale and consumption of alcohol was sanctioned under the Volstead Act, providing fines of up to $1,000 for those caught defying the law, even the possibility of six months behind bars. Yet, Prohibition couldn't stop people from drinking, and, in fact, inspired the world's largest cocktail party just 90 miles off the country's shore.

Fly Pan Am to Cuba and you can be bathing in Bacardi in hours.

Sloppy Joe's opened in Havana just as the idiocy of Prohibition shuttered bars from New York to Los Angeles, welcoming thirsty Americans to the corner of Zulueta and Animas, one block north of Parque Central, for a menu of sandwiches, cigars, and legal booze in abundance. The former grocery store, furnished, as one New York writer described, "as up-to-date as a Tenth Avenue delicatessen," was stocked to the rafters with its own brand of twelve-year-old rum displayed in giant mahogany cabinets, selling either by the bottle or by the drink, in an atmosphere thick with laughter, music and cigar smoke.

WHERE THE GREAT OF THE WORLD AND THE NOT-SO-GREAT MEET DAILY.

To Americans, Havana was Sloppy Joe's. Tourists headed straight from cruise ships to Joe's, then right back. Joe himself had been turned into a legendary figure by the journalists who made his place their second home. Among the world's greats who dropped by for a sip were the Duke of Windsor, Jean-Paul Sartre, Errol Flynn, Gary Cooper, Clark Gable, Spencer Tracy, John Wayne, Frank Sinatra, and Greta Garbo. Sloppy Joe's adopted Ernest Hemingway after he adopted Cuba, where the expatriate novelist lived for more than two decades.

COCKTAIL ARTS.

Sloppy Joe's drinks were anything but ordinary. In fact, most were inventive, served with unrivaled panache by the staff of elite barmen, guided by Fabio Delgado Fuentes, the "Father of all Cocktail Makers," and member of the *Club de Cantineros* (Association of Professional Cuban Barmen). During his employment at Sloppy Joe's, Senior Fuentes is said to have invented 33 world-class cocktails, as well as popularizing such native classics as the Cuba Libre, named for the war cry of the independence army who fought to free Cuba from the Spanish colonial yoke in the early wars of independence. It was his version of "El Draque," a drink of the working-class in Cuba as far back as the early 19th century, that helped the Mojito attain the status of high art and inspired the offspring Mint Julep.

A.K.A. Sloppy Joe's.

Curiously, Hemingway was responsible for a bit of plagiarism. When Prohibition ended in 1933, a fellow by the name of Joe Russell opened a bar in Key West, Florida, called the Blind Pig, located in a rundown building that he leased for three dollars a week, selling fifteen-cent whiskeys and ten-cent shots of gin. After the addition of a dance floor, the name was changed to the Silver Slipper. It was Hemingway with his connection to both Havana and Key West who suggested that Russell change the name of his bar, one of Papa's favorite stateside watering holes, to Sloppy Joe's, borrowing on the fame of the Cuban original.

Proprietor José Abeal (pictured third from left).

Proprietor José Abeal (pictured leaning on bar).

JOSÉ ABEAL Y OTERO
"Sloppy Joe"

José Abeal immigrated from Spain to Cuba in 1904 and got his first job as a bartender. He worked behind bars in both New Orleans and Miami before returning to Havana and a café named the Greasy Spoon. With the help of business-man Valentin Garcia, Jose bought what was then a small grocery store and turned it into what would become Sloppy Joe's Bar. Legend has it that an American patron was responsible for the name: "Why, Joe, this place is certainly sloppy, look at the filthy water running from under the counter." From then on, the name "Sloppy Joe" stuck.

CRADLE OF THE MOJITO

It's been around for over a century, starting as the drink of the Cuban *campesino* — sugar, lime and mint added to take the rough edge off nasty, cheap rum. The Mojito is a fragrant clear drink, sort of sweet and sort of tart, with a natural charm. As delicious and aromatic as it is refreshing, a more complex Mojito with brisk, penetrating flavor is made with one of the dark, rich, aged Bacardi rums. Unlike the Daiquiri, with its aura of sophistication, the Mojito is everyman's drink — rich, poor, and in-between.

Drinking a Mojito is like wearing a badge of Cubanness, a display and emblem of national pride. A sugarless Mojito, originally developed for our distinguished patron, Ernest Hemingway, who could not digest raw sugar, is made with cherry liqueur and grapefruit juice. Besides fresh mint, a Sloppy Joe's Mojito is always served with a strip of lime peel spiraled down through the glass (like the lemon peel in a Horse's Neck).

RUM
DRINKS

MOJITO

1 Teaspoonful of powdered sugar.
One half of a Lime.
1 Jigger of Soberano Cognac.
Chilled seltzer water.
4 Leaves of Mint.

Place the mint leaves into a collins glass and squeeze the juice from the lime over it. Add the powdered sugar, then gently smash the mint into the lime juice and sugar with a muddler. Add cracked ice, then add the rum and stir, and top off with the seltzer (or club soda). Garnish with the mint sprig and a strip of lime peel.

MOJITO No. 2

1 Teaspoonful of powdered sugar.
One half of a Lime.
Jigger of Gordon's Gin.
Chilled seltzer water.
4 Leaves of Mint.

Place the mint leaves into a collins glass and squeeze the juice from he lime over it. Add the powdered sugar, then gently smash the mint into the lime juice and sugar with a muddler. Add cracked ice, then add the rum and stir, and top off with the seltzer (or club soda). Garnish with the mint sprig and a strip of lime peel.

MOJITO No. 3

1 Teaspoonful of powdered sugar.
One half of a Lime.
1 Jigger of Soberano Cognac.
Chilled seltzer water.
4 Leaves of Mint.

Place the mint leaves into a collins glass and squeeze the juice from the lime over it. Add the powdered sugar, then gently smash the mint into the lime juice and sugar with a muddler. Add cracked ice, then add the rum and stir, and top off with the seltzer (or club soda). Garnish with the mint sprig and a strip of lime peel.

———

MOJITO CABALLITO

1 Teaspoonful of powdered sugar.
One half of a Lime.
Jigger of White Rum.
4 ounces Dry Vermouth.
Chilled seltzer water.
4 Leaves of Mint.

Place the mint leaves into a collins glass and squeeze the juice from the lime over it. Add the powdered sugar, then gently smash the mint into the lime juice and sugar with a muddler. Add cracked ice, then add the rum and stir, and top off with the seltzer (or club soda). Garnish with the mint sprig and a strip of lime peel.

HEMINGWAY SPECIAL

1 Jigger of White Rum.
1 Jigger of Grapefruit Juice.
1 Teaspoonful of Maraschino Liqueur.
One half of a Lime.
Chilled seltzer water.
4 Leaves of Mint.

Place the mint leaves into a collins glass and
squeeze the juice from the lime over it.
Gently smash the mint into the lime juice
with a muddler. Add cracked ice, then add
the rum and stir, and top off with the seltzer
(or club soda). Garnish with the mint sprig
and a strip of lime peel.

RUM COLLINS

1 Jigger of White Rum.
The juice of a Lime.
1 Teaspoonful of Powdered Sugar.
Chilled seltzer water.

Add cracked ice to a tall glass, then stir in the rum, lime juice, and sugar. Top off with the seltzer (or club soda).

SANTIAGO

1 Jigger of White Rum.
Juice of one Lime.
1 Teaspoonful of Powdered Sugar.
2 or 3 Drops of Grenadine Syrup.

Shake with cracked ice, strain and serve in cocktail glass.

MARY PICKFORD

1 Jigger of White Rum.
2 Jiggers of Pineapple Juice.
2 or 3 Drops of Maraschino Liqueur.
2 or 3 Drops of Grenadine Syrup.

Shake with cracked ice, strain and serve in cocktail glass with a wedge of fresh pineapple.

KAL KATZ

1 Jigger of White Rum.
1 Jigger of Dry Vermouth.
1 Jigger of Pineapple Juice.
2 or 3 Drops of Maraschino Liqueur.
2 or 3 Drops of Green Creme de Menthe.

Shake with cracked ice, strain and serve in cocktail glass.

CUBAN PRESIDENT

1 Jigger of White Rum.
1 Jigger of Dry Vermouth.
2 or 3 Drops of Orange Curacao.
2 or 3 Drops of Grenadine Syrup.

Shake with cracked ice, strain and serve in cocktail glass
with a peel of orange and a cherry.

AMERICAN PRESIDENT

1 Jigger of White Rum.
1 Jigger of Dry Vermouth.
The juice of a Lime.
2 or 3 Drops of Orange Curacao.
2 or 3 Drops of Grenadine Syrup.

Shake with cracked ice, strain and serve
in cocktail glass with a cherry.

RUM DAISY

1 Jigger of White Rum.
1/2 Teaspoon of Yellow Chartreuse.
1/2 Teaspoonful of Powdered Sugar.
1/2 Unsqueezed Lime Peel.
1 Dash of Angostura Bitters.

Add ingredients to a tall glass filled with cracked ice.
Stir and serve with a sprig of fresh mint and two cherries.

CHAPARRA

1 Jigger of Rum.
1 Jigger of Red (Sweet) Vermouth.
1/2 Teaspoonful of Powdered Sugar.

Add to cracked ice. Do not shake. Strain
and serve in cocktail glass with a lemon peel
in the shape of a spiral.

PLANTER'S PUNCH

1 Jigger of Dark Rum.
The juice of a Lime.
2 or 3 Drops of Orange Curacao.
2 or 3 Drops of Grenadine Syrup.

Shake with cracked ice, and serve in a julep glass
with ice and tropical fruit.

COLONEL BATISTA ESPECIAL

1 Jigger of White Rum.
1 Jigger of Dry Vermouth.
The juice of a Lime.
1/2 Teaspoonful of Powdered Sugar.
2 to 3 Drops of Grenadine Syrup.

Shake with cracked ice, strain and serve in
cocktail glass with a wedge of fresh
pineapple and 2 cherries.

NATIONAL COCKTAIL

1 Jigger of White Rum.
1/2 Jigger of Apricot Brandy.
1 Jigger of Pineapple Juice.

Shake with cracked ice, strain and serve in cocktail glass
with a wedge of fresh pineapple and 2 cherries.

MOFUCO COCKTAIL

1 Jigger of Rum.
1 Teaspoonful of Powdered Sugar.
1 Dash of Angostura Bitters.
1 Unsqueezed peel of a Lime.
1 Egg.

Shake with cracked ice, strain and serve in cocktail glass.

RUM COCKTAIL

1 Jigger of White Rum.
1/2 Teaspoon of Orange Curacao.
1/2 Teaspoonful of Powdered Sugar.
1/2 Unsqueezed Lime Peel.
1 Dash of Angostura Bitters.

Shake lightly with cracked ice, strain and serve in cocktail glass with a sprig of fresh mint.

PRESIDENTE MENOCAL SPECIAL

1 Jigger of White Rum.
1 Teaspoonful of Powdered Sugar.
The juice of half a Lime.
4 Leaves of Fresh Mint.

Place the mint leaves into a julep glass with the sugar and lime juice. Gently smash with a muddler. Fill the glass with crushed ice, then add the rum and stir. Garnish with a sprig of fresh mint sprig and 2 cherries.

JAI ALAI SPECIAL

1 Jigger of White Rum.
1/2 Jigger of White Creme de Cacao
1/2 Jigger of Orange Juice.
The juice of half a Lime.

Shake with cracked ice, strain and serve in cocktail glass.

CUBA LIBRE

1 Jigger of White Rum.
The juice of half a Lime.
Coca-Cola.

Fill a high-ball glass with cracked ice and half fill with cola. In a cocktail shaker, combine rum and lime, add ice and shake. Strain the mixture over the cola.

JABON CANDADO
(Ramoncito Lopez Especial)

1 Jigger of White Rum.
1 Teaspoonful of Powdered Sugar.
The juice of half a Lime.
1/2 of the white of an Egg.

Shake with cracked ice, strain and serve in cocktail glass.

HAVANA BEACH SPECIAL

1 Jigger of White Rum.
1 Jigger of Pineapple Juice.
1 Teaspoonful of Powdered Sugar.

Shake with cracked ice, strain and
serve in cocktail glass.

HAVANA CLUB

2 Jiggers of White Rum.
1 Jigger of Dry Vermouth.

Stir ingredients with cracked ice in a mixing glass.
Strain into a Manhattan glass, squeeze a lemon peel
over the top, and serve with the peel in the glass.

GOLDEN GLOVE

1 Jigger of Dark Rum.
1 Teaspoonful of Cointreau.
1 Teaspoonful of Powdered Sugar.
The juice of half a Lime.

Shake in an electric shaker with crushed ice, squeeze
an orange peel over the top, and serve as a frappe
with the peel in the glass.

BACARDI FLIP

1 Jigger of White Rum.
1 Teaspoonful of Powdered Sugar.
1 Egg.

Shake with cracked ice, strain and serve in cocktail glass with powdered cinnamon on top.

HAVANA SPECIAL

1 Jigger of White Rum.
1 Jigger of Pineapple Juice.
2 to 3 Drops of Maraschino Liqueur.

Shake with cracked ice, and pour into a tall glass filled with crushed ice. Garnish with tropical fruit.

TROPICANA

1 Jigger of White Rum.
2 Jiggers of Pineapple Juice.
1 Jiggers of Grapefruit Juice.
2 or 3 Drops of Grenadine Syrup.

Shake with cracked ice, and pour into a tall glass filled with crushed ice. Garnish with a wedge of fresh pineapple.

ISLA DE PINOS
(Isle of Pines)

1 Jigger of White Rum.
2 Jiggers of Grapefruit Juice.
1 Teaspoonful of Powdered Sugar.

Shake with cracked ice, and pour into a tall glass filled with crushed ice. Garnish with a grapefruit slice and 2 cherries.

CUBAN MANHATTAN

2 Jiggers of White Rum.
1 Jigger of Red (Sweet) Vermouth.
2 or 3 Dashes of Angostura Bitters.

Stir ingredients with cracked ice in a mixing glass.
Strain into a Manhattan glass and add a cherry.

CUBA BELLA

1 Jigger of White Rum.
1/2 Jigger of White Creme de Menthe.
1 Jigger of Orange Juice.
2 or 3 Drops of Grenadine Syrup.

Shake with cracked ice, and pour into a
tall glass filled with crushed ice. Garnish
with an orange slice and 2 cherries.

DAIQUIRI No. 1

1 Jigger of White Rum.
1 Teaspoonful of Powdered Sugar.
The juice of half a Lime.

Shake with cracked ice, strain and serve in cocktail glass.

DAIQUIRI No. 2

1 Jigger of White Rum.
1 Teaspoonful of Orange Juice.
2 or 3 Drops of Orange Curacao.
1 Teaspoonful of Powdered Sugar.
The juice of half a Lime.

Shake with cracked ice, strain and serve in cocktail glass.

DAIQUIRI No. 3

1 Jigger of White Rum.
1 Teaspoonful of Maraschino Liqueur.
1 Teaspoonful of Grapefruit Juice.
1 Teaspoonful of Powdered Sugar.
The juice of half a Lime.

Shake with cracked ice, strain and serve in cocktail glass.

DAIQUIRI No. 4
(Florida Style)

1 Jigger of White Rum.
1 Teaspoonful of Maraschino Liqueur.
1 Teaspoonful of Powdered Sugar.
The juice of half a Lime.

Shake in an electric shaker with crushed ice, and serve as a frappe.

GIN
DRINKS

GIN MOJITO

1 Teaspoonful of powdered sugar.
One half of a Lime.
1 Jigger of Gin.
Chilled seltzer water.
4 Leaves of Mint.

Place the mint leaves into a collins glass and squeeze the juice from the lime over it. Add the powdered sugar, then gently smash the mint into the lime juice and sugar with a muddler. Add cracked ice, then add the gin and stir, and top off with the seltzer (or club soda). Garnish with the mint sprig and a strip of lime peel.

IDEAL COCKTAIL

1 Jigger of Gin.
1/2 Jigger of Dry Vermouth.
1/2 Jigger of Grapefruit Juice.
2 or 3 Drops of Maraschino Liqueur

Shake with cracked ice, strain and serve in cocktail glass with a cherry.

BRONX

1 Jigger of Gin.
1 Jigger of Dry Vermouth.
1 Jigger of Red (Sweet) Vermouth.
1/2 Teaspoonful of Orange Curacao.
1 Teaspoonful of Orange Juice.

Shake with cracked ice, strain and serve in cocktail glass with a slice of orange.

BRONX No. 2

1 Jigger of Gin.
1 Jigger of Dry Vermouth.
1 Jigger of Red (Sweet) Vermouth.
1/2 Teaspoonful of Orange Curacao.

Add to cracked ice. Do not shake. Stir and strain into a cocktail glass with a peel of lemon and 2 cherries.

FLAMINGO

1 Jigger of Gin.
1/2 Jigger of Apricot Nectar Liqueur
The juice of half a Lime.
1 Teaspoonful of Grenadine Syrup.

Shake with cracked ice, strain and serve in cocktail glass.

FLAMENCO COCKTAIL

1 Jigger of Gin.
1/2 Jigger of Apricot Brandy
The juice of half a Lime.
1 Teaspoonful of Grenadine Syrup.

Shake with cracked ice, strain and serve in cocktail glass.

TOM COLLINS

1 Jigger of Gin.
1 Teaspoonful of Powdered Sugar.
The juice of a Lemon.
Seltzer Water.

Fill a hi-ball glass with cracked ice. Add gin, sugar and lemon juice, and stir. Fill with seltzer water and serve.

GIN RICKEY

1 Jigger of Gin.
The juice of a Lemon.
Seltzer Water.

Fill a hi-ball glass with cracked ice. Add gin and lemon juice, and stir. Fill with seltzer water and serve.

GIN FIZZ

1 Jigger of Gin.
1 Teaspoonful of Powdered Sugar.
The juice of a Lemon.
Seltzer Water.

Fill a hi-ball glass with cracked ice. Add gin, sugar and lemon juice, and stir. Fill with seltzer water and serve.

GIN COCKTAIL

2 Jiggers of Gin.
2 or 3 Drops of Orange Curacao.
1 Dash of Angostura Bitters.

Add to cracked ice. Do not shake. Stir, then strain and serve in cocktail glass with a peel of lemon.

GIN SLING

1 Jigger of Gin.
Ginger Ale.

Fill a hi-ball glass with cracked ice. Add gin, then
fill with ginger ale and serve with a peel of lemon.

GIN BLUE

1 Jigger of Gin.
1 Jigger of Parfait Amour.
1 Teaspoonful of Powdered Sugar.
The juice of half a Lemon.

Shake with cracked ice, strain and
serve in cocktail glass.

MARTINI
(Seco)

1 Jigger of Gin.
1/2 Jigger of Dry Vermouth.
2 Dashes of Orange Bitters.

Add to cracked ice. Do not shake. Stir, allowing it to get very cold, then strain and serve in cocktail glass with a peel of lemon.

MARTINI
(Demi-Seco)

1 Jigger of Gin.
1 Jigger of Dry Vermouth.
2 Dashes of Orange Bitters.

Add to cracked ice. Do not shake. Stir, allowing it to get very cold, then strain and serve in cocktail glass with an olive.

GOLDEN FIZZ

1 Jigger of Gin.
The juice of a Lemon.
1 Teaspoonful of Powdered Sugar.
1 Yolk of an Egg.

Shake with cracked ice, strain and serve in cocktail glass.

———

GREEN FIZZ

1 Jigger of Gin.
2 or 3 Drops of Green Creme de Menthe.
The juice of a Lemon.
Teaspoonful of Powdered Sugar.
White of an Egg.

Shake with cracked ice, strain and
serve in cocktail glass.

ROYAL FIZZ

1 Jigger of Gin.
2 or 3 Drops of Grenadine Syrup.
The juice of a Lemon.
1 Teaspoonful of Powdered Sugar.
1 Egg.

Shake with cracked ice, strain and serve in cocktail glass.

NEW ORLEANS FIZZ

1 Jigger of Gin.
2 or 3 Drops of Green Creme de Menthe.
1 Jigger of Cream of Milk.
1/2 Teaspoonful of Powdered Sugar.
1 White of an Egg.
2 or 3 Drops of Kirsch.

Shake with cracked ice, strain and serve in cocktail glass.

RAIMUND'S GIN FIZZ

1 Jigger of Gin.
2 or 3 Drops of Grenadine Syrup.
2 or 3 Drops of Orange Blosson Water.
1 Jigger of Cream of Milk.
1 Teaspoonful of Powdered Sugar.
1 White of an Egg.
The juice of half a lemon.

Shake with cracked ice, and serve in tall glass.

SILVER FIZZ

1 Jigger of Gin.
The juice of a Lemon.
1 Teaspoonful of Powdered Sugar.
1 White of an Egg.

Shake with cracked ice, strain and
serve in cocktail glass.

DUBONNET COCKTAIL

2 Jiggers of Dubonnet
1 Jigger of Gin.

Shake with cracked ice, strain and serve in
cocktail glass with a peel of lemon.

ORANGE BLOSSOM

1 Jigger of Gin.
1 Teaspoonful of Powdered Sugar.
The juice of half an Orange.

Shake with cracked ice, and serve in tall glass.

CLOVER LEAF

1 Jigger of Gin.
The juice of half a Lemon.
2 or 3 Drops of Grenadine Syrup.
2 or 3 Drops of Orange Curacao.
1 White of an Egg.

Shake with cracked ice, and serve in tall glass
with a sprig of fresh mint.

CLOVER CLUB

1 Jigger of Gin.
The juice of half a Lemon.
1 Teaspoonful of Powdered Sugar.
1 White of an Egg.

Shake with cracked ice, and serve in tall glass.

SINGAPORE SLING

1 Jigger of Gin.
1 Jigger of Cherry Brandy.
1 Jigger of Benedictine.
Seltzer Water (on the side)

Shake with cracked ice, then strain into a tall glass
filled with cracked ice. Fill to individual taste with
seltzer or club soda.

ALEXANDER

1 Jigger of Gin.
1/2 Jigger of Dark Creme de Cacao.
1/2 Jigger of Cream of Milk.

Shake with cracked ice, strain and serve in cocktail glass.

BROWNS

1 Jiggers of Gin.
1/2 Jigger of Dry Vermouth.
1/2 Jigger of Red (Sweet) Vermouth.
1 Teaspoonful of Powdered Sugar.
The juice of half an Orange.

Shake with cracked ice, and serve in tall glass.

MORNING GLORY

1 Jigger of Gin.
The juice of a Lemon.
1 Egg.
2 or 3 Drops of White Creme de Menthe.

Shake with cracked ice, and serve in tall glass.

SEIBERLING

1 Jigger of Gin.
1/2 Jigger of Dry Vermouth.
1 White of an Egg.
The juice of a Lemon.
1 Drop of Maraschino Liqueur.

Shake with cracked ice, and serve in tall glass.

AUNT EMILY COCKTAIL

1 Jigger of Gin.
1 Jigger of Apple Jack.
1/2 Jigger of Apricot Brandy.
The juice of half an Orange.
2 or 3 Drops of Grenadine Syrup.

Shake with cracked ice, and serve in tall glass.

JOAN BLONDELL COCKTAIL

1 Jigger of Gin.
1 Jigger of Dry Vermouth.
1 Jigger of Benedictine.
2 or 3 Drops of Absinthe.
1 Dash of Angostura Bitters.

Shake with cracked ice, strain and serve in cocktail glass.

BLUE MOON

2 Jiggers of Gin.
1 Jigger of Parfait Amour.

Shake with cracked ice, strain and serve in cocktail glass.

S.O.S. COCKTAIL

1 Jigger of Gin.
1 Jigger of Dry Vermouth.
1 Jigger of Red (Sweet) Vermouth.

Add to cracked ice. Do not shake. Stir, then strain
and serve in cocktail glass with a wedge of fresh
pineapple and 2 cherries.

SNOW BALL

1 Jigger of Gin.
1 Jigger of Parfait Amour.
1/2 Jigger of Green Creme de Menthe.
2 Jiggers of Fresh Milk.

Shake with cracked ice, strain and serve
in cocktail glass.

PALM OLIVE

1 Jigger of Gin.
2 Jiggers of Grapefruit Juice.
1/2 Teaspoonful of Green Cream de Menthe.

Shake with cracked ice, and serve in tall glass.

SAN MARTIN

1 Jigger of Gin.
1 Jigger of Dry Vermouth.
1 Jigger of Red (Sweet) Vermouth.
1 Teaspoonful of Anisette.
1 Dash of Angostura Bitters.

Wet the brim of a cocktail glass with lemon and coat
with powdered sugar. Shake ingredients with cracked
ice, strain and serve in the glass.

RUBY SLIPPER COCKTAIL

1 Jigger of Sloe Gin.
1 Jigger of Cherry Brandy.
The juice of a Lemon.
1/2 White of an Egg.

Shake with cracked ice, strain and serve in cocktail glass.

SEVILLANA

1 Jigger of Gin.
1 Jigger of Red (Sweet) Vermouth.
1/2 Teaspoonful of Orange Curacao.
1/2 Teaspoonful of Powdered Sugar.
1 Dash of Angostura Bitters.

Add to cracked ice. Do not shake. Stir, then strain and serve in cocktail glass with a peel of lemon and 2 cherries.

PEPIN RIVERO

1 Jigger of Gin.
1 Jigger of White Creme de Cacao.
1/2 Jigger of Cointreau.
1 Jigger of Fresh Milk.
1/2 Teaspoon of Powdered Sugar.

Shake with cracked ice, strain and serve in cocktail glass.

ROSE

1 Jigger of Gin.
1 Jigger of Calvados.
1 Jigger of Dry Vermouth.
1/2 Teaspoon of Grenadine Syrup.

Shake with cracked ice, strain and
serve in cocktail glass.

MISS JOAN KETCHUM
SPECIAL COCKTAIL

1 Jigger of Gin.
1 Jigger of Pineapple Juice.
1 Teaspoonful of Apricot Brandy.
1 Teaspoonful of Grenadine Syrup.

Shake with cracked ice, strain and serve in cocktail glass.

MENDIETA
SPECIAL COCKTAIL

1 Jigger of Gin.
1 Jigger of Dry Vermouth.
1 Jigger of Red (Sweet) Vermouth.
1 Teaspoonful of Orange Curacao.

Shake with cracked ice, strain and serve in cocktail glass
with a peel of orange and 2 cherries.

MARCO-ANTONIO

1 Jigger of Gin.
1 Jigger of Grapefruit Juice.
1 Teaspoonful of Maraschino Liqueur.
1 Teaspoonful of Grenadine Syrup.
1/2 White of an Egg.

Shake with cracked ice, strain and serve in cocktail glass.

GOLDEN DAWN

1 Jigger of Gin.
1 Jigger of Calvados.
1/2 Jigger of Apricot Brandy.
1 Teaspoonful of Orange Juice.
1/2 Teaspoonful of Grenadine Syrup.

Shake with cracked ice, strain and serve
in cocktail glass with a cherry.

GIN DAISY

2 Jiggers of Gin.
1/2 Teaspoonful of Yellow Chartreuse.
1 Dash of Angostura Bitters.
1/2 Teaspoonful of Powdered Sugar.

Add to cracked ice. Do not shake. Stir and
serve in a hi-ball glass with a cherry.

OLD SMUGGLER'S AWAKEN

1 Jigger of Gin.
1 Teaspoonful of Powdered Sugar.
1 Dash of Angostura Bitters.
1 Egg.

Shake with cracked ice, strain and serve in cocktail glass
with a peel of lemon and a dusting of powdered cinnamon.

DELIO NUNEZ

1 Jigger of Gin.
1 Jigger of Grapefruit Juice.
1/2 Teaspoonful of Powdered Sugar.
1 Teaspoonful of Maraschino Liqueur.
1/2 White of an Egg.

Line the bottom of a cocktail glass with the egg white.
Shake other ingredients with cracked ice, and strain
into the glass.

CAFFERY
SPECIAL COCKTAIL

1 Jigger of Sloe Gin.
1 Teaspoonful of Apricot Brandy.
1 Teaspoonful of Orange Juice.
1/2 Teaspoonful of Grenadine Syrup.

Shake with cracked ice, and serve in hi-ball
glass with a wedge of fresh pineapple and 2
cherries.

SLOE GIN RICKEY

1 Jigger of Sloe Gin.
The juice of a Lemon.
Seltzer Water.

Serve in a hi-ball glass filled with cracked ice.

SLOE GIN FIZZ

1 Jigger of Sloe Gin.
1/2 Teaspoonful of Orange Curacao.
1/2 Teaspoonful of Amer Picon.
1/2 Teaspoonful of Powdered Sugar.
The juice of half a Lemon.

Shake with cracked ice, strain and serve in cocktail glass.

SEVENTH HEAVEN

1 Jigger of Sloe Gin.
1 Jigger of Red (Sweet) Vermouth.
1/2 Teaspoonful of Fernet-Branca.
1/4 Teaspoonful of Powdered Sugar.

Shake with cracked ice, strain and serve in cocktail glass with peel of a lemon and several almonds or walnuts.

MARY MORANDEYRA

1 Jigger of Sloe Gin.
1 Jigger of Red (Sweet) Vermouth.
1 Jigger of Grapefruit Juice.
1 Teaspoonful of Maraschino Liqueur.

Shake with cracked ice, strain and serve in cocktail glass.

EUREKA

1 Jigger of Sloe Gin.
1 Jigger of Calvados.
1 Teaspoonful of Cherry Brandy.
1 Teaspoonful of Lemon Juice.

Shake with cracked ice, strain and serve in cocktail glass.

DIAMOND HITCH

1 Jigger of Gin.
1 Dash of Angostura Bitters.
Champagne.

Fill a hi-ball glass with cracked ice, and add gin and bitters.
Fill the glass to the brim with Champagne.

MIAMI BEACH SPECIAL

1 Jigger of Gin.
2 Jiggers of Pineapple Juice.
1 Teaspoonful of Powdered Sugar.

Shake with cracked ice, strain and serve in cocktail glass.

CHIC

1 Jigger of Sloe Gin.
1 Jigger of Red (Sweet) Vermouth.
1 Jigger of Grapefruit Juice.
1 Teaspoonful of Maraschino Liqueur.

Shake with cracked ice, strain and serve in cocktail glass with a few almonds.

DOUGLAS FAIRBANKS

2 Jiggers of Gin.
1 Jigger of Apricot Brandy.
The Juice of a Lemon.
1 White of an Egg.

Shake with cracked ice, strain and serve in cocktail glass.

HORSE'S NECK

1 Jigger of Gin.
1 Dash of Angostura Bitters.
Champagne.

Fill a hi-ball glass with cracked ice. Add 1 Jigger of Gin, garnish with a long spiral of lemon peel draped over the edge, and serve with a bottle of ginger ale.

AZIZ SPECIAL

1 Jiggers of Gin.
1 Teaspoonful of Powdered Sugar.
The juice of a Lemon.
2 Jiggers of Fresh Milk.
White of an Egg.
2 Dashes of Orange Flower Water.

Shake with cracked ice, strain and serve in cocktail glass.

BIRD OF PARADISE

1 Jiggers of Gin.
2 Teaspoonfuls of Raspberry Syrup.
The juice of a Lime.
2 Jiggers of Fresh Milk.
White of an Egg.

Shake with cracked ice, strain and serve
in cocktail glass with a rose petal float.

VERMOUTH DRINKS

COLONIAL

2 Jiggers of Red **(Sweet)** Vermouth.
1 Jigger of Gin.
1 Teaspoonful of Powdered Sugar.
2 or 3 Drops of Amer Picon.
2 or 3 Drops of Orange Curacao.
1 Dash of Angostura Bitters.

Shake with cracked ice, and serve in hi-ball glass.

AMERICAN VERMOUTH

2 Jiggers of Red **(Sweet)** Vermouth.
2 or 3 Drops of Amer Picon.
2 or 3 Drops of Orange Curacao.

Shake with cracked ice, strain and serve
in cocktail glass with a cherry.

BLIND GEN

2 Jiggers of Red (Sweet) Vermouth.
1 Yolk of an Egg.

Shake with cracked ice, strain and serve in cocktail glass.

"REX" SPECIAL

2 Jiggers of Red (Sweet) Vermouth.
2 or 3 Dashes of Angostura Bitters.
Seltzer Water.

Fill a tall glass with cracked ice, and add the vermouth and bitters. Add seltzer and serve with a peel of lemon.

PARIS MIDI

2 Jiggers of Dry Vermouth.
1 Jigger of Creme de Cassis.
Seltzer Water.

Fill a tall glass with cracked ice, and add the vermouth
and cassis. Add seltzer and serve with a peel of lemon.

CASIANO COCKTAIL

2 Jiggers of Red (Sweet) Vermouth.
1 Teaspoonful of Creme de Cassis.

Shake with cracked ice, strain and serve in
cocktail glass with a peel of lemon.

ADONIS COCKTAIL

1 Jigger of Red (Sweet) Vermouth.
2 Jiggers of Dry Sherry.
1 Dash of Orange Bitters.

Add to cracked ice. Do not shake. Stir, allowing it to get very cold, then strain and serve in cocktail glass.

BAMBOO COCKTAIL

1 Jigger of Dry Vermouth.
2 Jiggers of Dry Sherry.
1 Dash of Angostura Bitters.

Add to cracked ice. Do not shake. Stir, allowing it to get very cold, then strain and serve in cocktail glass.

COGNAC
DRINKS

ERROL FLYNN'S
PICK ME UP

1 Jigger of Martell Cognac.
1 Jigger of Dubonet.
2 or 3 Drops of Anisette.
1 White of an Egg.

Shake with cracked ice, strain and serve in cocktail glass.

SIDE CAR

The Juice of a Lemon.
1 Jigger of Martell Cognac.
1/2 Jigger of Cointreau.

Shake with cracked ice, strain and serve in cocktail glass.

STINGER

1 Jigger of Fine Cognac
1 Jigger of White Creme de Menthe

Shake with cracked ice, strain and serve in cocktail glass.

BETTY ROSS

1 Jigger of Martell Cognac.
1 Jigger of Port Wine.
2 or 3 Drops of Orange Curacao.
2 or 3 Dashes of Angostura Bitters.

Shake with cracked ice, strain and serve
in cocktail glass.

JACK ROSE

The Juice of half a Lemon.
2 Jiggers of Apple Jack.
2 or 3 Drops of Grenadine.

Shake with cracked ice, strain and serve in cocktail glass.

SOBERANO
BRANDY HIGHBALL

1 Jigger of Martell Cognac.
Mineral Water.

Add Cognac to a tall glass filled with cracked ice.
Fill to the brim with Mineral Water.

MC AVOY

1 Jigger of Martell Cognac.
1 Scoop of Vanilla Ice Cream, melted.

Shake with cracked ice, strain and serve in cocktail glass.
Serve with a dusting of powdered cinnamon.

MORNING STAR

1 Jigger of Martell Cognac.
1 Jigger of Port Wine.
1 Dash of Angostura Bitters.
1 Teaspoonful of Powdered Sugar.
1 Egg.

Shake with cracked ice, strain and serve
in cocktail glass. Serve with a dusting of
powdered cinnamon.

MENDEZ VIGO
SPECIAL

1 Jigger of Martell Cognac.
1 Teaspoonful of Powdered Sugar.
1 Teaspoonful of Maraschino Liqueur.
The Juice of half a Lemon.

Shake with crushed ice in an electric shaker
and serve as a frappe.

JOSEPHINE BAKER

1 Jigger of Martell Cognac.
1 Jigger of Port Wine.
1 Jigger of Apricot Brandy.
1 Teaspoonful of Powdered Sugar.
1 Yolk of an Egg.
1 Lemon Peel, squeezed.

Shake with cracked ice, strain and serve in cocktail glass.
Serve with a dusting of powdered cinnamon.

CHANTECLAIR

1 Jigger of Martell Cognac.
1 Jigger of Dry Vermouth.
1 Teaspoonful of Orange Curacao.

Add to cracked ice. Do not shake. Strain and serve in cocktail glass with two cherries.

HOT-KISS

1 Jigger of Martell Cognac.
1 Jigger of Red (Sweet) Vermouth.
1 Teaspoonful of Orange Curacao.

Add to cracked ice. Do not shake. Stir, then strain and serve in cocktail glass with two cherries.

CALEDONIA

1 Jigger of Martell Cognac.
1 Jigger of Creme de Cacao.
1 Jigger of Milk.
1 Yolk of an Egg.
1 Dash of Angostura Bitters.
1 Lemon Peel, squeezed.

Shake with crushed ice, strain and serve in cocktail glass.
Serve with a dusting of powdered cinnamon.

CLEOPATRA

1 Jigger of Martell Cognac.
1 Jigger of Port Wine.
1/2 Jigger of Cointreau.
1/2 Jigger of Pineapple Juice.

Shake with cracked ice, strain and serve in cocktail glass.

BLUE PARADISE

1 Jigger of Martell Cognac.
1 Jigger of Dubonnet.
1/2 Jigger of Parfait Amour.
1 Lemon Peel, squeezed.

Shake with cracked ice, strain and serve in cocktail glass.

BLUE MOON

1 Jigger of Martell Cognac.
1 Jigger of Creme de Violette.
1 Teaspoonful of Blue Curacao.

Shake with cracked ice, strain and serve
in cocktail glass.

BRANDY DAISY

2 Jiggers of Martell Cognac.
1/2 Teaspoonful of Yellow Chartreuse.
1 Dash of Angostura Bitters.
1 Lemon Peel, squeezed.

Shake with cracked ice, strain and serve in cocktail glass
with two cherries and a few sprigs of fresh mint.

BRANDY COCKTAIL

2 Jiggers of Martell Cognac.
1/2 Teaspoonful of Orange Cauacao.
1/2 Teaspoonful of Powdered Sugar.
1 Dash of Angostura Bitters.
1 Lemon Peel, squeezed.

Shake with cracked ice, strain and serve in cocktail
glass with a sprig of fresh mint.

BRANDY FLIP

1 Jigger of Martell Cognac.
1 Tablespoon of Powdered Sugar.
1 Egg.

Shake with cracked ice, strain and serve in cocktail glass.
Serve with a dusting of powdered cinnamon.

BETWEEN-SHEETS

1 Jigger of Fine Cognac.
1 Jigger of Creme de Cacao.
1 Jigger of Sweet Cream.
1 Teaspoonful of Powdered Sugar.
1 Dash of Angostura Bitters.
1 Lemon Peel, squeezed.

Shake with cracked ice, strain and serve
in cocktail glass.

A B C COCKTAIL

1 Jigger of Fine Cognac.
1 Jigger of Port Wine.
1/2 Jigger of Maraschino Liqueur.
1/2 Teaspoonful of Powdered Sugar.
1 Dash of Angostura Bitters.

Shake with cracked ice, strain and serve in cocktail
glass with two cherries and a few sprigs of fresh mint.

MINT JULEP
(Mexican Style)

1 Jigger of Fine Cognac.
1 Teaspoonful of Powdered Sugar.
1 Tablespoon Natural Water.
Fresh Mint Leaves.

Crush a few mint leaves in the bottom of a julep glass,
then fill with crushed ice. Add sugar, water, and cognac.
Stir gently until glass frosts. Garnish with a fresh mint
sprig.

VERSAILLES CLUB

1 Jigger of Fine Cognac.
1 Jigger of Dubonnet.
1/2 Teaspoonful of Orange Curacao.

Add ingredients to a mixing glass filled with cracked ice.
Do not shake. Stir, then strain into a cocktail glass
and serve with a lemon peel.

EGG-NOG

1 Jigger of Fine Cognac.
3 Jiggers of Fresh Milk.
1 Teaspoonful of Powdered Sugar.
2 Eggs.

Shake with cracked ice, strain and serve
in cocktail glass.

CAFE COCKTAIL

1 Jigger of Fine Cognac.
1 Jigger of Dark Creme de Cacao
1 Teaspoonful of Powdered Sugar.
2 Jiggers of Black Coffee

Shake with cracked ice, strain and serve in cocktail glass with a peel of lemon.

MORNING DOCTOR

1 Jigger of Cognac.
1 Cup of Fresh Milk.
1 Teaspoonful of Powdered Sugar.

Beat with an egg beater and serve in a tall glass.

KILROY'S BRACER

1 Jigger of Cognac.
The juice of a Lime.
1 Egg.
3 Dashes of Angostura Bitters.
½ Teaspoonfull of Anisette.

Shake with cracked ice, then strain into
a tall glass filled with cracked ice. Fill
to individual taste with seltzer or club soda.

WHISKEY
DRINKS

MINT JULEP

1 Jigger of Bourbon Whiskey.
1 Teaspoonful of Powdered Sugar.
1 Tablespoon Natural Water.
Fresh Mint Leaves.

Crush a few mint leaves in the bottom of a julep glass, then fill with crushed ice. Add sugar, water, and bourbon. Stir gently until glass frosts. Garnish with a fresh mint sprig.

MINT JULEP
(Virginia Style)

1 Jigger of Rye Whiskey.
1 Teaspoonful of Powdered Sugar.
1 Tablespoon of Lemon Juice.
Fresh Mint Leaves.

Crush a few mint leaves in the bottom of a julep glass, then fill with crushed ice. Add sugar, lemon juice, and rye. Stir gently until glass frosts. Garnish with a fresh mint sprig.

MILLIONAIRE

1 Jigger of Rye Whiskey.
1 White of an Egg.
2 or 3 Drops of Grenadine Syrup.
2 or 3 Drops of Orange Curacao.

Shake with cracked ice, and serve in tall glass.

APPLE JACK

1 Jigger of Apple Jack.
1 Teaspoonful of Powdered Sugar.
The juice of a Lemon.
2 or 3 Drops of Orange Curacao.

Shake with cracked ice, strain and
serve in cocktail glass.

MANHATTAN
(Seco)

1 Jigger of Rye Whiskey.
1 Jigger of Dry Vermouth.
1 Dash of Angostura Bitters.

Add ingredients to a mixing glass filled with cracked ice. Do not shake. Stir until it becomes very cold, strain and serve with a lemon peel in a Manhattan glass.

———

MANHATTAN
(Dulce)

1 Jigger of Rye Whiskey.
1 Jigger of Red (Sweet) Vermouth.
1/2 Teaspoonful of Orange Curacao.

Add ingredients to a mixing glass filled with cracked ice. Do not shake. Stir until it becomes very cold, strain and serve with a cherry in a Manhattan glass.

WHISKEY SOUR

1 Jigger of Canadian Whiskey.
1 Teaspoonful of Powdered Sugar.
The juice of a Lemon.

Shake with cracked ice, strain and serve in cocktail glass.

ZAZERAC

1 Jigger of Rye Whiskey.
1 Teaspoonful of Powdered Sugar.
2 or 3 Drops of Absinthe.
1 Dash of Angostura Bitters.
1 Dash of Orange Bitters.

Fill a hi-ball glass with cracked ice.
Add ingredients, stir, add mineral water
and a peel of lemon.

SMOKED COCKTAIL

1 Jigger of Scotch Whiskey.
1/2 Teaspoonful of Orange Curacao.
1 Teaspoonful of Powdered Sugar.
Juice of half a Lemon.

Shake with cracked ice, strain and serve in cocktail glass.
Garnish with sprig of fresh mint.

SUMMER WELLES
SPECIAL COCKTAIL

1 Jigger of Canadian Whiskey.
1 Jigger of Red (Sweet) Vermouth.
1/2 Teaspoonful of Orange Curacao.
1/2 Teaspoonful of Powdered Sugar.
1 Dash of Angostura Bitters.

Shake with cracked ice, strain and serve in cocktail glass.
Garnish with sprig of fresh mint and green cherries.

MILK PUNCH

1 Teaspoonful of Powdered Sugar.
1 Jigger of Rye Whiskey.
2 Jiggers of Milk.

Shake with cracked ice, strain and serve in cocktail glass.

OLD FASHIONED

1 Jigger of Rye Whiskey.
1 Teaspoonful of Powdered Sugar.
2 or 3 Dashes of Angostura Bitters.
2 or 3 Drops of Orange Curacao.
1 Slice of Lemon.
1 Slice of Orange.
1 Cherry.

Place sugar in the bottom of an Old Fashioned glass. Add bitters, curacao and fruit, and muddle together until the sugar is dissolved. Fill glass with cracked and add the rye.

SPECIALTY
COCKTAILS

ABSINTHE DRIP

3/4 Jigger of Absinthe.
1/4 Jigger of Anisette.

Serve with ice in a French Absinthe glass.

———

SWET SET

1 Jigger of Absinthe.
1/2 Jigger of Dry Vermouth.
1 Teaspoonful of Powdered Sugar.
1 White of Egg.

Shake with cracked ice, strain and serve in a coupe.

BUTTERFLY
(Absinthe Frappe)

3/4 Jigger of Absinthe.
1/4 Jigger of Anisette.

Shake with crushed ice in an electric shaker and serve as a frappe.

MY-SIN COCKTAIL

1 Jigger of Absinthe.
1 Jigger of Anisette.
1 White of an Egg.

Wet a cocktail glass with Lemon Juice and dust with Powdered Sugar. Shake with cracked ice, strain and serve into the glass.

POUSSE CAFE

1/4 Jigger of Creme de Cacao.
1/4 Jigger of Benedictine.
1/4 Jigger of Anisette.
1/2 Jigger of Brandy.

Carefully pour each ingredient with a teaspoon into a cordial glass to create colored layers.

RAINBOW PLUS

1/8 Jigger of Grenadine.
1/8 Jigger of Anisette.
1/8 Jigger of Parfait Amour.
1/8 Jigger of Green Creme de Menthe.
1/8 Jigger of Orange Curacao.
1/8 Jigger of Yellow Chartreuse.
1/8 Jigger of Green Chartreuse.
1/8 Jigger of Jamaica Rum.

Carefully pour each ingredient with a teaspoon into a cordial glass to create colored layers.
Burn upon serving.

AUGUI COCKTAIL

1 Jigger of Fine Cognac.
1 Jigger of Dry Vermouth.
1 Jigger of Gin.
2 or 3 Drops of Grenadine Syrup.
2 or 3 Drops of Orange Curacao.
The juice of a Lemon.

Shake with cracked ice, strain and serve in cocktail glass.

MIAMI

1 Jigger of Gin.
2 Jiggers of Pineapple Juice.

Shake with cracked ice, and serve in tall glass.

HELEN
TWELVETREES

1 Jigger of Gin.
2 Jiggers of Pineapple Juice.
2 or 3 Drops of Parfait Amour.

Shake with cracked ice, and serve in tall glass.

———

DOCTOR SPECIAL

2 Jiggers of Gin.
1 Jigger of Apple Jack.
2 or 3 Drops of Grenadine Syrup.
2 or 3 Drops of Orange Bitters.

Shake with cracked ice, strain and
serve in cocktail glass.

SLOPPY JOE'S

1 Jigger of Fine Cognac.
2 Jiggers of Pineapple Juice.
1 Jigger of Port Wine.
2 or 3 Drops of Grenadine Syrup.
2 or 3 Drops of Orange Curacao.

Shake with cracked ice, and serve in tall glass.

———

HAVANA

1 Jigger of Rum.
2 Jiggers of Pineapple Juice.

Shake with cracked ice, and serve in tall glass.

JOAN BENNETT

2 Jiggers of Rum.
2 Jiggers of Pineapple Juice.
1 Jigger of Parfait Amour.

Shake with cracked ice, and serve in tall glass.

LAVIN

1 Jigger of Rum.
1 Jigger of Dry Vermouth.
1 Jigger of Pineapple Juice.
2 or 3 Drops of Grenadine Syrup.
2 or 3 Drops of Orange Curacao.

Shake with cracked ice, and serve in tall glass.

PANAMA MAIL

1 Jigger of Gin.
1 Jigger of Dry Vermouth.
1 White of an Egg.
2 or 3 Drops of Cassis.

Shake with cracked ice, and serve in tall glass.

MANUEL SPECIAL

1 Jigger of Fine Cognac.
Jiggers of Dry Vermouth.

Shake with cracked ice, strain and serve in cocktail glass with a cherry and a peel of lemon.

AROUND
THE WORLD

1 Jigger of Gin.
1/2 Jigger of Green Creme de Menthe.
2 Jiggers of Pineapple Juice.

Shake with cracked ice, and serve in tall glass.

KENTUCKY

1 Jigger of Rye Whiskey.
2 Jiggers of Pineapple Juice.

Shake with cracked ice, and serve in tall glass.

NEW YORK

1 Jigger of Fine Cognac.
2 Jiggers of Pineapple Juice.

Shake with cracked ice, and serve in tall glass

VALDES

1 Jigger of Gin.
2 Jiggers of Pineapple Juice.
2 or 3 Dashes of Angostura Bitters.

Shake with cracked ice, and serve in tall glass.

TEQUILA
COCKTAIL

1 Jigger of Tequila.
1 Teaspoonful of Powdered Sugar.
The juice of a Lemon.
1 Dash of Angostura Bitters

Shake with cracked ice, strain and serve in cocktail glass.

PORTO FLIP

3 Jiggers of Port Wine.
1 Teaspoonful of Powdered Sugar.
1 Egg.

Shake with cracked ice, strain and serve in cocktail glass with a dusting of powdered cinnamon.

CHAMPAGNE PUNCH
(For Six Persons)

1 Jigger of Maraschino Liqueur.
2 Jiggers of Fine Cognac.
1 Jigger of Red Curacao (or Strawberry Liqueur)
Half a bottle of Champagne.
One quarter bottle of Mineral Water.
The peels of 4 Lemons.

Sweeten to taste and serve in Champagne coupes.

CHAMPAGNE COCKTAIL

Place a lump of sugar in a Champagne coupe with a peel
of lemon and a leaf of fresh mint. Add a few drops of
Angustura Bitters and Orange Curacao.
Fill the glass with Champagne

CIDER PUNCH

1 Jigger of Maraschino Liqueur.
2 Jiggers of Fine Cognac.
1 Jigger of Red Curacao (or Strawberry Liqueur).
Half a bottle of Cider.
One quarter bottle of Mineral Water.
The peels of 4 lemons.

Sweeten to taste and serve in Champagne coupes.

CIDER COCKTAIL

Place a lump of sugar in a Champagne coupe with a
peel of lemon and a leaf of fresh mint. Add a few
drops of Angustura Bitters and Orange Curacao.
Fill the glass with Cider.

BLACK VELVET

1 Part Guinness Stout Beer.
1 Part Champagne.

Fill a tall champagne flute halfway with chilled stout,
then floating the sparkling wine on top

Good FOOD

...although it enjoys high priority among the delights of man, is the enemy of strong drink. In the tradition of Sloppy Joe's, we offer only the following. It is our hope it will interfere only slightly with your blessed drunkenness.

SANDWICH LIST

CHICKEN

TURKEY

HAM-EGGS

ANCHOVIES

SARDINES

CAVIAR

COMBINATION

SLOPPY-SPECIAL

ROQUEFORT-CHEESE

SWISS-CHEESE

CREAM-CHEESE

LIVER

BOLOGNA-SAUSAGE

SLICES-AND EVERY THING

INDEX

RUM DRINKS

GIN DRINKS

VERMOUTH DRINKS

COGNAC DRINKS

WHISKEY DRINKS

SPECIALITY COCKTAILS

MEMORANDUM

MEMORANDUM

MEMORANDUM

MEMORANDUM

MEMORANDUM

MEMORANDUM

MEMORANDUM

MEMORANDUM

MEMORANDUM

IN HAVANA

EVERYTHING STARTS FROM

SLOPPY JOE'S
BAR

THE GREATEST MEETING
PLACE OF THE GLOBE

●

SLOPPY JOE'S OFFERS TO VISITORS
THE LARGEST ASSORTMENT OF THE

**CUBAN RUMS and
IMPORTED LIQUORS**
AT WHOLESALE PRICES

**WHERE QUALITY OF PRODUCTS
IS GUARANTEED BY THE HOUSE**

Made in the USA
Charleston, SC
28 January 2010